COUPLES STUDY GUIDE

$\mathcal{F}$RIENDS
&
$\mathcal{L}$over$s$

COUPLES STUDY GUIDE

FRIENDS & Lovers

by Mitch and Jan Mitchell

DPI

DISCIPLESHIP
PUBLICATIONS
INTERNATIONAL

One Merrill Street
Woburn, MA 01801
1-888-DPI-BOOK
Fax: (617) 937-3889

Friends and Lovers: Couples Study Guide
©1996 by Discipleship Publications International
One Merrill Street, Woburn, MA 01801

Printed in the United States of America

Cover design & illustration: Chris Costello
Interior layout: Chris Costello and Laura Root

ISBN 1-57782-005-3

Contents

Acknowledgments

Jan and I would personally like to thank Sam and Geri Laing for the tremendous help we have received in our marriage, our family and our ministry. You are both very dear to us and have truly been a Godsend in our lives. Sam, I respect you as a deeply spiritual man of God, as a "friend who sticks closer than a brother" and as a prophet who has taken Triangle Church deeper and higher. Geri, you are my closest sister in the Lord, the sister I never had growing up. Your elegance, grace and laughter, combined with total devotion to Sam, your family and the Lord, is an upward call to women all over the world. Jan and I love you both deeply.

Mitch

An Introductory Word from Sam and Geri Laing

We wrote *Friends & Lovers* not only with the aim of giving couples a higher ideal of marriage, but with the purpose of helping them to actually have a better one in real life. With the completion of this study guide by Mitch and Jan Mitchell, a powerful tool is now available for helping couples do just that.

Use this study guide as it was intended—read it, evaluate your own strengths and weaknesses as a husband or wife, and then sit down with your spouse and work together toward a better marriage. (We suggest that each of you keep a separate notebook in which you write your responses to the questions.) The book itself will be limited in impact if you do not as a couple bring its teachings and principles to life in your marriage. As a matter of fact, it could add to your frustrations by making you see what could be, but what is not yet attained. Any serious effort on your part as a couple to discuss the concepts in the book will itself bring some great results.

Mitch and Jan Mitchell are dear friends to us and are very special people in God's kingdom. They were leading the Triangle Church when we moved to North Carolina in 1993, and they generously stepped aside and took the place as our right-hand couple. Without their willingness and humility, we could not have come here. And without their friendship, support and partnership, we could not have built the church that we have. We are happy for you to get to know them through this workbook, and we hope that their insights, love for God and love for each other will come through loud and clear as they help you build a greater marriage.

PART

1

·Relationship·

CHAPTER 1

Friends and Lovers

Put aside your preconceptions, your problems and your past. Above all, get rid of your low expectations.... The only thing stopping you is your doubt. It is time to lay faithlessness aside and get on with the business of building your marriage. (p. 21)

1. Do you deeply trust God at this point in your life? Do you struggle with doubt, discouragement and discontentment? Decide to "begin again" with God, expecting great victories. See Romans 8:28-39.

2. As you begin this upward call to an awesome marriage, do you *believe* God will help you change personally in your marriage? Discuss this together before moving forward. Make a *godly pact* to repent of doubt and halfhearted effort and to give yourselves totally to God and to each other.

Our spouses should be our best friends on earth. They should know our minds, hearts, souls and feelings more than anyone else does. (p. 22)

3. Do you feel this *soul-mate unity* in your marriage? Do you really know each other? On a scale of 1 to 10, how close are you to each other? What do you as an individual need to change to become a better friend to your spouse? What do both of you need to do together to be best friends?

4. Read and study together Ecclesiastes 4:9-12. What have you personally accomplished with your life so far? What have you both accomplished in your marriage? Discuss together where your marriage is on your priority list based on the time, energy and effort put into it.

> Unfortunately, there are many who claim leadership of God's people, but have failed at home. The Bible disqualifies them as true leaders, because who they are at home is who they really are. (p. 24)

5. Read and study together 1 Timothy 3:1-13 and Titus 1:5-9, 2:1-8. There is a desperate need in the kingdom of God for more spiritual leadership. Help each other pick out two or three areas you individually need to grow in to become more of what God wants you to be.

6. Are you individually happy with the sexual relationship in your marriage? Men, you cannot be lovers without being friends! Women, you cannot be friends without being lovers! Do you both agree this is God's plan? Decisions must be made now to humbly listen to each other and work together for mutual joy, happiness and fulfillment.

7. Are you and your wife creating an awesome family? Is your marriage relationship contributing positively to the strength, spirituality and happiness of your children? Make a list of the attributes you both want to build into your family. How will you both carry this out? Remember the old adage: "Plan the work, then work the plan!"

8. Reread Chapter One and summarize here the decisions you both have made. Put them on your prayer list and review them daily. Look for God to answer specific prayers about your marriage. Take note of the answers and personal changes God is allowing you both to make. Share them with others.

CHAPTER 2

Can We Talk?

How is the communication going in your marriage? Do you know and understand your spouse? Do you talk on a deep level, or do you limit your conversation to the superficial and mundane? Do you find yourself holding in what you would like to say? Are you frustrated? Are you afraid to talk about what is most important? Do you have difficulty putting your thoughts and feelings into words? Do you find that you are not even sure what your feelings and thoughts are? Is your idea of an open exchange limited to having an intense conversation? When is the last time you had a heart-to-heart discussion [that is, before beginning this study guide] with your spouse that was more than an angry scene? Are there things you have lied about to your spouse or deliberately withheld from him or her? How often do you just sit down and talk? (p. 28)

1. Read through the above questions. You as a couple need to provide thoughtful answers. Make some obvious resolutions in the space below, knowing there is more specific help on the way. Examples of resolutions could be

   • I resolve to be painfully open with my wife/husband.
   • We will be a team from this day forward.
   • I will be her/his #1 supporter.
   • Truth is the foundational building block of my marriage. I will love, listen to, speak and follow the truth from this day forward.

Let's face it: It is usually men who hold back in communication....Men who think they have nothing to talk about are deceived....*There is no man anywhere who does not need to open his heart to his wife, whether he feels the need or not.* (pp. 28-29)

2. Just For Men! From firsthand experience, I strongly suggest an intense study of Proverbs on the following concepts: arrogance (arrogant), pride (proud), stiff-necked, foolish, stubborn (stubbornness), humble (humility) and listen(ing). Get help from your wife in these areas. She knows you the best and will be *very happy* to help you out! Get your quiet time journal and go to work for a while. I personally spent several months on these and other related topics.

3. Take note of the ten communication killers on pages 30-37:

   1. Failure to listen
   2. Defensive listening
   3. Disrespect of viewpoint
   4. Cutting, critical remarks
   5. Hinting
   6. Clamming up
   7. Blowing up
   8. Grumbling, griping & complaining
   9. Lying
   10. Distractions

Each of you should individually reread this section (pp. 30-37) and on a scale of 1 to 10 put a number by each communication killer first for yourself and second for your spouse. The numbers represent the following:

1   We need others to help us on this one.
3   Let's work on this together first.
5   O.K., but O.K. always means improvement is needed.
7   I'm satisfied now; let's work on the "1"s and "3"s.
9   Awesome; we can help someone else out.
10   "Celebrate, celebrate, dance to the music. .."

Compare notes and discuss what you learned from your spouse. (For example, why did you as a husband put "9" for #6 (Clamming up) and your wife put "1" for you? This is a definite point for discussion!)

4. Now is not the time to get overwhelmed! Let your spouse pick one or two communication killers for you to work on and then focus on them for a month. Evaluate each other at the end of a month and decide to continue with the focused choices or pick one or two others to work on. And I quote,

> Now we know what *not* to do. But just reading through the list will not change your marriage. You must take these things seriously. You must treat them as a threat to your relationship and make sure they are put out of your life. (p. 37)

5. Now study together the ten building blocks of great communication on pages 38-47:

1. Seek to synchronize
2. Spend special sessions
3. Be refreshingly real

4. Learn the levels
5. Lighten up
6. Speak silently
7. Show common courtesy
8. Share the spiritual
9. Practice the praise principle
10. Faithfully forgive

This time each of you should, on a scale of 1 to 10, put a number by each building block, one for you and one for your spouse (husband for the wife, wife for the husband). Again, compare and talk about the differences and pick one or two building blocks to focus on. Reevaluate monthly.

CHAPTER 3

When a Man Loves a Woman

The Bible's emphasis is not on rules but on a role model. It does not provide some*thing* to do, but some*one* to imitate. There is a marriage relationship in which the husband is the perfect example. A man can look at this husband and be completely confident in imitating his life and example. Who is this husband? *Jesus.* Who is his wife? *The church.* (p. 50)

1. For husbands: Ephesians 5:21-6:3 must be studied, *re*studied, *re*searched, *re*dedicated to until it becomes reality! Make a list of Jesus' attitudes toward the church. Are these your attitudes toward your wife? Your children? Make a personal decision to ask yourself, "What would Jesus do?" " H o w would he handle this situation?"

2. Husband, what is your personal conviction about your leadership as the man in your household? Wife, what is your conviction? Are you both unified with the Bible (Ephesians 5:23; 1 Corinthians 11:3)? Discuss this with each other and other qualified Christian counselors if help is needed.

3. Let us take note of the six aspects of a husband's love for his wife on pages 53-61:

    1. An unselfish love
    2. A sensitive love
    3. An exclusive love
    4. An initiating love
    5. A love without bitterness
    6. A considerate love

4. Husband, I encourage you to get help in each of these areas from your wife. Let her fill in the following blanks with specific things you can do that help her feel special and radiant.

    a) An unselfish love

    b) A sensitive love

    c) An exclusive love

    d) An initiating love

    e) A love without bitterness

    f) A considerate love

CHAPTER 4

R-E-S-P-E-C-T

...the wife must respect her husband.

EPHESIANS 5:33

1. Wife, what does it mean to your husband to be respected by you? Ask how you can honor, revere and appreciate him more.

> The attitude of respect for a husband that the Scriptures urge upon the wife must be followed up with the action of submission to his leadership. To do anything less is either to rebel directly against what God has said or is to merely give it lip-service. Submission is the *practical outworking of respect in real life* (italics added). (p. 65)

2. Submission is defined in the original Greek language as "to line up under." What is your personal definition and conviction?

3. Sit down with your husband and discuss page 66: "What Submission Is Not and What Submission Is." Ask your husband what he needs the most from you in order to work together as a united team.

4. Study the following scriptures together and consider both of your attitudes toward submission. Get help from others if needed: Philippians 2:6-11; Ephesians 5:24; 1 Thessalonians 5:12; Hebrews 13:17; 1 Peter 2:13-17.

5. If either of you feels there is abuse, weak leadership or continuing disrespect, decide what you must do to change the situation.

6. Which of these five encouragements does your husband need the most?

   1. Believe in him
   2. Focus on his good qualities
   3. Praise him
   4. Seek to adapt and to please
   5. Help others to respect him

Let him tell you specifically what he needs to feel respected and followed by you. Write down what he tells you for future reference. (Then actually *refer* to it in the future!)

One More Thought...

You wives must learn to *adapt* yourselves to your husband as you submit yourselves to the Lord.

Wives *adapt* yourselves to your husbands that your marriage may be a Christian unity (Ephesians 5:22; Colossians 3:18 —J.B. Phillips translation, emphasis added).

1. Do I *accept* and build my life around the man I married?
2. Am I *devoted* to my husband?
3. Do I *appreciate* him for who he is?
4. Do I focus on the *positive* in him or the negative?
5. Do I *trust* God that we can continually grow to be what God intends?

Ask your husband for his answers to the above questions.

A-CCEPT
D-EVOTE
A-PPRECIATE
P-OSITIVE
T-RUST

PART

2

·Romance·

CHAPTER 5

The Plan

In the midst of our failure there is a simple, profound truth that gives hope: *God has a plan.* It is not just a good plan. It is the best plan, and it works without fail. We can understand it, and we can follow it. (pp. 80-81)

1. For this plan to work, you must first deal with any sin or worldliness in your personal lives. Is there any lust, pornography (magazines, videos, movies, cybersex), masturbation, sexual immorality or adultery that must be dealt with? Do not let this chance go by without a decision and a commitment to change and get help from others if need be.

2. Do you both agree that married sex is good, beautiful, wonderful, satisfying, needful, natural and noble? Discuss with your spouse.

3. Do you both agree that sexual activity with any person other than your marriage partner is wrong? Discuss with your spouse.

Married sex gets better at the years go by. (p. 83)

4. Do you both agree that this should be the case? Is it true in your marriage?

CHAPTER 6

The Problems

1. Which phrase best describes your sexual relationship?

    1. Function without fulfillment
    2. Fizzle, not sizzle
    3. Fighting, not fun
    4. Fading frequency
    5. Fanning the flames

It would be best to answer this question individually and compare answers afterwards. Talk out your differences, be humble, and decide to be united.

> Failure to recognize these problems is extremely dangerous. If you accept any of them as the norm, you are inviting disaster....To adequately deal with these problems, we must go beyond the symptoms and discover and eradicate their underlying causes. (p. 85)

2. Study together the problems described on pages 86-100. For each problem ask yourself: "Is this issue a problem in our sex life?" Ask your spouse: "What do I need to change to make things better?"

Afterwards, write down your response to each area below with the important thoughts, feelings and decisions that you both make after your study and discussion of this important section.

Discuss each problem area thoroughly before going on to the next one. Make sure both of you have been open and humble. God will reward your communication.

a) Pattern of neglect

b) Pain from the past

c) Pregnancy

d) Progeny

e) Purity lost

f) Punishment

g) People and phones

h) Physical differences

i) Poor understanding of expectation

3. Finally:

> TALK! Don't make your partner be a mind
> reader.... The higher your expectations, the more
> urgent it is for you to communicate, because greater
> will be your disappointment if your expectations
> are not fulfilled. (p. 100)

CHAPTER 7

The Promise

1. Now is the time to have fun! Put the kids to bed (if you have any). Go to your bedroom and lock the door. Light the candles. Put on the romantic music. And...open your Bible to Song of Songs! Read Song of Songs all the way through together. The husband reads all the sections entitled "Lover" to his wife. The wife reads all the sections entitled "Beloved" back to her husband in response. You can read together all the sections entitled "Friends." The more you dramatize with Shakespearean accent, ambience and amorousness the better it will be. Have fun!

2. You should now discuss the seven positive steps to building a great love life found on pages 101-111:

   a) Attitude

   b) Attention

   c) Affection

d) Atmosphere

e) Attractiveness

f) Attire, aroma and allure

g) Articulation

3. On a scale of 1 to 10 write down how you honestly feel you are doing in these areas. Then write down how your spouse is doing in these areas.

     1 He/she needs help from others.
     3 We need to talk.
     5 I'm happy, are you?
     7 We're getting better all the time.
     9 Unbelievably awesome.
    10 Unspeakable ecstasy!

4. Take notes from your discussion. Do not get overwhelmed or depressed—neither of these responses is a biblical sign of repentance. (See 2 Corinthians 7:10-11.) Pick out one or two areas that are the most important to your spouse and work on those first. Reevaluate monthly.

One More Thought...

Sexual love is a great gift of God to be enjoyed and cherished for a lifetime. While the passion and excitement of a new marriage is a tremendous joy and a memory to be cherished forever, nothing can compare to a love that has been enjoyed and practiced for a very long time....Enjoy and celebrate your life together! (p. 113)

1. Do you enjoy and cherish your life together?

2. Decide to bring passion and excitement back into your marriage.

3. Answer the following question: "How can we specifically enjoy and celebrate our sexual love together?" Celebration means festivity, fiesta, gala, party, a happening, etc....Now that's a romance created in the image of God. Go for it!

PART

3

·Reality·

CHAPTER 8

It's Only Money

...there are three reasons God gives us material blessings. First, he gives them to us to sustain our lives and the lives of our children. Second, he gives us money that it may be used to advance his kingdom. And last, he gives us our financial resources that we might help the poor and practice hospitality. All of these are good and righteous purposes. (p. 117)

1. Do you both agree that God gives us material possessions for the three reasons stated above? What are your personal convictions on this? Are you united?

2. Are these the three areas where your money is really going? How are your decisions about where to spend your money affecting your marriage?

3. Is your handling of money causing a love for it, a source of conflict between you, or a continual source of anxiety for either of you?

4. Study together the following ten attitudes toward finances. Rate yourself on a scale of 1 (poor) to 10 (great) on these attitudes. Ask your spouse to rate you as well. Share your thoughts with each other and be humble!

    a) Establish the right priorities:
       Matthew 6:24,33; Proverbs 23:4-5

    b) Live within your means:
       Proverbs 22:26-27, 24:27; Philippians 4:11-13

    c) Design and stick with a budget:
       Proverbs 16:3-9, 21:30; Psalm 37:3-5

    d) Put God's work first in your budget:
       Malachi 3:8-12; Leviticus 27:30

    e) Avoid credit buying: Proverbs 22:7

    f) Pay bills on time: Romans 13:8

    g) Listen to advice: Proverbs 12:15, 13:10, 19:20

h) Work hard and build a solid financial base:
Proverbs 13:11, 20:4, 22:29, 28:19;
Ephesians 4:28; 1 Thessalonians 4:11-12

i) Set aside some of your income in a savings account:
Proverbs 6:6-8

j) Be generous:
Proverbs 11:24-25, 19:17, 23:6-7, 28:22,27

5. Decide to be painfully honest as you both evaluate which areas you need to tackle first. Write down your goals and decisions under each of the ten attitudes. Hold each other accountable and get help from other qualified disciples.

6. Study together the ten steps to financial freedom and answer the following questions as you put together a workable budget:

a) What is your total income each month?

b) What are your fixed expenses each month?

c) What are the variable expenses you can standardize?

d) Put a rough budget together allowing for the husband's personal allotment as well as the wife's allotment to run the household. What will these allotments be? Do you both agree?

e) List all credit cards, loans, personal debts, etc. Have you eliminated credit card spending (unless you pay it off at the end of the month)? Have you eliminated ATM cards (if you tend to be irresponsible in your use of them)?

f) How will you attack your debt? Are you paying off smaller bills first? Now is the time to discuss "necessities" versus "luxuries." What about cable TV, long distance phone calls, a car (or two cars), health clubs, child care costs vs. second job, etc.?

g) How much will your contribution be? Do you have plans for special missions contributions? Study 2 Corinthians 8:1-7, 9:6-11.

h) Have you set up a savings account? How much will go into it each month?

i) Which spouse will manage the checkbook? Who has the most expertise? Which one will handle it with the most accountability and the least amount of stress?

j) Do you need outside help? You must make this a top priority.

CHAPTER 9

Peace Accord

Peace in marriage is not intended only for a select few—it is what God wants all of us to enjoy. It is something that we must seek, treasure and work for. It is something that we must expect and never be satisfied until we obtain. (p. 135)

1. Study James 3:17-18 together as a couple. What are some of the reasons for marital conflict found in this passage? What are some biblical avenues toward marital peace? How does this passage apply to you as a husband or as a wife?

2. Study the five causes of conflict on pages 136-139. How do they apply to you? Discuss at length and decide which one you need to focus on to help your spouse the most.

    a) A prideful attitude:
       Proverbs 13:10, 1 Peter 5:5

    b) A critical spirit:
       Proverbs 22:10, 27:15-16; Philippians 4:8

    c) A defensive posture:
       Proverbs 17:19, 18:13

d) Inflammatory words:
Proverbs 15:1, 12:18, 29:11

e) Unresolved issues and feelings:
Ephesians 4:25-27

3. Study together the eight cures for conflict found on pages 139-143. Ask your spouse to pick out the ones you need to work on. Use these steps the next time conflict arises between you. Hold each other accountable and reevaluate monthly.

a) Search for truth. What is the truth?

b) Apologize first. Without excusing or minimizing, honestly ask for forgiveness.

c) Find common ground. What are our points of agreement?

d) Sharpen the focus. What are the real issues at hand?

e) No side issues. Are we dealing with only one issue at a time?

f) Forgive completely. (Colossians 3:13; Luke 23:34)

g) Work through the healing process. Ask yourself: Do I push the buttons of healing, devotion and affection or the buttons of hurt, selfishness and separation?

h) Get help! This is the wisdom behind the church! God expects us to get help from other disciples with experience in these areas. Ask yourself: "Am I getting help? Am I encouraging my husband/wife to get help, or am I discouraging him or her?"

CHAPTER 10

In the Long Run

1. Is your marriage better off today than it has ever been in the past? Discuss together.

2. What gets in the way of making your marriage a top priority? Make a list (examples: job(s), kids, hobbies, in-laws, energy level, financial stress, etc.) and determine to make changes where needed.

> In the book of Revelation, Jesus chides the church in Ephesus for losing her first love (Revelation 2:4). Have you lost your first love for your spouse? Have you lost the excitement, joy and wonder of your early days? Where is the heady anticipation and mystery that was yours on your wedding day? Does your heart beat faster when you see each other across a room anymore? Do you still give those special knowing looks that say you care?... [Jesus'] solution? He called upon them to remember the height from which they had fallen. He urged them to repent (change their attitude) and do the things they did at first. (p. 146)

3. Answer together the above questions. Decide together: We will repent of any attitudes that cause disunity, and we will renew our love for each other.

4. How do you as a couple respond to trials? Do you draw inward and isolate yourselves from each other? Do you get depressed, overwhelmed and discouraged? Do you drag each other down with bad attitudes? Do you rely on each other for strength and encouragement? Do you help each other develop character and dependency on God?

5. Study together Ecclesiastes 4:12; Philippians 3:12-16; 2 Corinthians 3:18; 1 Thessalonians 4:9-10; Hebrews 6:1-2; 2 Peter 3:18. Remember the "divine triangle" that you form with God being the point at the top and the two of you being the points at the bottom. You must both make personal decisions to continue to grow spiritually or your marriage will never be what God originally intended!

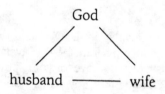

6. List separately your five closest friends. Come together and compare your lists. Answer the following questions:

> How many other married people have you allowed into your real life? What other married friends of yours know the real scoop on the two of you? With how many couples have you had strong words, difficult confrontations, angry feelings and tearful conversations and have continued being friends?...Do any of these people live in close proximity to you now? Are they consistently involved in your life? (p. 150)

7. Are there any unresolved problems from your past (previous to your marriage)? Are there any unresolved problems in your marriage now? If need be, get help from qualified disciples!

8. Are you as a husband/wife individually and as a team using your talents for the Lord and his kingdom or for worldly pursuits? Discuss this with other disciples who know you well. Study together Romans 12; 1 Corinthians 12;1 Peter 4:7-11, and find your special niche in the kingdom.

CHAPTER 11

Up from Defeat

We recount these stories with the purpose of giving hope. We tell them so that all of us can see that no matter how bad things may be, there is a way out. We began this book with a statement of three convictions, and we want to end with them as well:

- Any two people can change.
- Any marriage can be fixed.
- Any marriage can become great.

(p. 165)

1. You have just finished reading in Chapter 11 six real-life stories. All of these couples have been given a new start, a new hope, a new vision and a new life. This happened through the grace and power of God and the principles laid out in *Friends & Lovers*. What would your story be? Sit down together and write down changes you have made, goals you have set for yourself and your marriage while working through this book. Continue to keep this as a journal of your adventure through life and the awesome ways God is leading you and your marriage. What do you do now? Continue to grow and reevaluate your progress. Listen to your spouse. Have fun. And if you have kids...get a copy of the Laing's book entitled *Raising Awesome Kids in Troubled Times*.

One More Thought...

R-ejoice always.
E-njoy each other.
A-dversity will come.
L-earn to love and comfort.
I-will always remain positive.
T-rue happiness comes from within.
Y-ou can do it—together!

Consider each of the above statements. Which one most describes your weakness? Your strength?

Epilogue

Bottom line, marriage is all about selflessness. It is being willing to put your own self aside for the good of another person. Luke 9:24 is the great paradox of life: Lose your life and you will find it. Long-term fulfillment will never come without unselfish sacrifice. This is a fact of life and is a bedrock principle of marriage. (p. 170)

As we close, do you see the need to rededicate yourselves to God and to your love for him? (Matthew 22:37-40). Each of you should decide personally to be the very best disciple you can be. Pride and selfishness in their many facets and forms are still your #1 and #2 enemies.

Courtship, Dating and Engagement *

1. Study and evaluate your relationships as singles based on the six tests for a serious relationship on pages 174-181:

   a) The test of spirituality: Answer the questions on page 174. Do a thorough study of 1 Corinthians 7:39; 2 Corinthians 6:14; Ezra 9:1-4.

   b) The test of compatibility: Is there a deep love for this sister? Do I really respect and want to follow this brother? Is our compatibility obvious to others who are deeply spiritual?

   c) The test of purity: Is our relationship based primarily on physical attraction? Is our relationship pure? Is there anything we are doing or have done in showing affection that has violated the Scriptures or our consciences? Are we open with others about our purity?

   d) The test of longevity: How much time have we given God to work in this relationship? Have we dated other people to make sure?

* Since this workbook was designed for married couples, singles will not likely be using it. For that reason, this section (and this section alone) may be copied for their use as they read and apply the appendix of *Friends & Lovers*. We encourage you to copy it and give it to those who need it.

e) The test of society: Who really knows us as a dating couple? Have we spent any time with married couples who can help us?

f) The test of economy: Are our career, financial, family, etc. goals compatible? Have we discussed these with others who can help?

Friends & Lovers

SCRIPTURE REFERENCES

(in order of their appearance)

Chapter 4

Proverbs 31:12
Ephesians 5:33
Ephesians 5:22-24
Philippians 2:6-11
Ephesians 5:24
1 Thessalonians 5:12
Hebrews 13:17
1 Peter 2:13-17
1 Samuel 25
Ephesians 5:22 J.B. PHILLIPS
Colossians 3:18 J.B. PHILLIPS

Chapter 5

Genesis 1:31
Genesis 2:25
Genesis 3:1-17
Genesis 2:24
Genesis 1:28
1 Timothy 3:1-7
1 Timothy 4:1-5
Titus 1:5-9
Hebrews 13:4
Romans 12:9
Romans 12:21
Matthew 19:4-6
Exodus 20:14
Mark 7:20-23
Romans 1:24-27
1 Corinthians 6:9-20
Hebrews 13:4

Chapter 6

Song of Songs 2:15
1 Corinthians 7:3-5
Isaiah 43:18-19
Exodus 20:13

1 Corinthians 6:19-20
Hebrews 13:4
Matthew 19:9
Proverbs 5:3-4, 7-8
Matthew 5:27-28
Proverbs 4:25
Matthew 5:29-30
Hebrews 4:15-16
Ephesians 4:26-27
Genesis 1:27

Chapter 7

Song of Songs 4:10
Luke 6:38
Philippians 2:4
Romans 15:3
Song of Songs 6:1
Song of Songs 1:2
Song of Songs 1:16-17
Song of Songs 5:14-15
Song of Songs 7:1,5
1 Corinthians 6:19
Song of Songs 4:1-5
Song of Songs 4:9-11
Song of Songs 5:3-5
Song of Songs 6:7
Song of Songs 5:10-16
Song of Songs 7:6
1 Corinthians 7:4
Song of Songs 4:12-5:1
Song of Songs 7:7-9
Ephesians 5:32

Chapter 8

Matthew 6:33
James 1:17
1 Timothy 4:4

1 Timothy 6:10
Matthew 6:24
Proverbs 23:4-5
Proverbs 22:26-27
Proverbs 24:27
Philippians 4:11-13
Proverbs 16:3
Malachi 3:8-12
Numbers 18:21
Leviticus 27:30
2 Corinthians 8 and 9
Proverbs 22:7
Romans 13:8
Proverbs 12:15
Proverbs 13:10
Proverbs 19:20
Proverbs 20:4
Proverbs 22:29
Proverbs 28:19
Proverbs 13:11
1 Timothy 6:9
Ephesians 4:28
1 Thessalonians 4:11-12
Proverbs 6:6-8
Proverbs 28:22,27
Proverbs 11:24-25
Matthew 5:45
Proverbs 23:6-7
Matthew 26:8-13
Proverbs 19:17
2 Corinthians 8:3-4
2 Corinthians 9:7

Chapter 9

James 3:17-18
Proverbs 27:17
Proverbs 17:1
Proverbs 13:10
1 Peter 5:5

Proverbs 22:10
Proverbs 27:15-16
1 Corinthians 13:5
Philippians 4:8
Proverbs 17:19
Proverbs 18:13
Proverbs 15:1
Proverbs 12:18
Proverbs 29:11
Ephesians 4:25-27
Proverbs 18:19
2 Corinthians 13:8
Proverbs 20:9
Proverbs 20:5
Colossians 3:13
Luke 23:34
Proverbs 15:31
Philippians 4:2-3

Chapter 10

Matthew 19:6
Luke 9:23
Revelation 2:4-7
Proverbs 18:24
Romans 5:3-4
James 1:2-4
Ecclesiastes 4:9-12
Philippians 2:1-4
Colossians 1:17
Philippians 3:12-16
2 Corinthians 3:18
1 Thessalonians 4:10
Hebrews 6:1-2
2 Peter 3:18
Proverbs 27:9
Proverbs 27:6
1 Corinthians 2:16
Hebrews 12:1
2 Corinthians 12:7-10

Galatians 2:11-14
Song of Songs 1:2
Romans 12:3,6
Isaiah 43:18-19

Chapter 11

Isaiah 41:18
Philippians 4:4
Romans 5:3-5
Philippians 4:8

Epilogue

Luke 9:23-24

Appendix

Proverbs 31:10
Romans 8:28
Matthew 6:33
Matthew 22:37-40
1 Corinthians 7:39
2 Corinthians 6:14
Ezra 9:1-4
Ephesians 5:22-25, 33
1 Thessalonians 4:3-8
1 Corinthians 7:4
1 Corinthians 6:19-20
2 Thessalonians 3:6-10
Genesis 24
1 Thessalonians 4:3-8
1 Corinthians 7:4
1 Corinthians 6:19-20
2 Thessalonians 3:6-10
Genesis 24